# Chit Chat

Activity Book **2**

**Paul Shipton**
Course consultant: Derek Strange

My name is

_____ .

This is my book.

**OXFORD**
UNIVERSITY PRESS

# Hello again!

**1** Read and match.

**a** What's your name?

**b** How are you?

**c** What's your favourite colour?

1  Red.

2 My name's Kim. ☐

3 I'm fine, thank you. ☐

**2** Write the names.

a t K

J t e

e i p k S

c i k N

**3** Read then colour the name cards in activity 2.

 SUPERSTARS
Kat's favourite colour is blue.

 Jet's favourite colour is red.

 Spike's favourite colour is green.

 Nick's favourite colour is purple.

**4** | Complete the answers.

elephant   Black
~~Peter~~   Yes   No   fine

1  What's your name?
   I'm <u>Peter.</u>

2  How are you?
   I'm _____, thank you.

3  What's your favourite colour?
   _____.

4  What's your favourite animal?
   An _____.

5  Do you like dogs?
   _____, I don't.

6  Do you like pizza?
   _____, I do.

**5** | Answer the questions in activity 4 about you.

# My star turn

1 _____   4 _____

2 _____   5 _____

3 _____   6 _____

# Music time!

**6** Read and match.

1 piano    C

2 trumpet

3 guitar

4 violin

5 drum

**7** Write **Yes, it is** or **No, it isn't**.

1 Is it a drum?

No, it isn't.

2 Is it a trumpet?

_____

3 Is it a violin?

_____

4 Is it a guitar?

_____

5 Is it a piano?

_____

**8** Match and write sentences.

Tig

Zig

Fig

Mig

1 <u>Tig can play the piano.</u>

2 _____

3 _____

4 _____

**9** Listen and chant. Then listen and repeat the words. 🔊 6

My little bed is red.
I've got a red hat.
My little pet is red.
I've got a red cat.

# 1 Sports time

**1** | Read and match.

1  I can skate.     a

2  I can dive.

3  I can't swim.

4  I can't ski.

5  I can swim.

**2** | Complete the sentences about you. Use **can** or **can't**.

1  I _____ skate.

2  I _____ dance.

3  I _____ dive.

4  I _____ swim.

5  I _____ ski.

**Find a photo. Stick your photo here.**

I can _____.

**3** Look at the chart. Write **Yes, I can** or **No, I can't**.

| Name |  skate | swim | football | basketball | tennis | hockey |
|------|------|------|------|------|------|------|
| Jet | ✓ | ✓ | ✓ | ✓ | ✓ | ✓ |
| Nick | ✓ | ✓ | ✗ | ✗ | ✓ | ✓ |
| Kat | ✓ | ✗ | ✓ | ✓ | ✗ | ✗ |
| Spike | ✗ | ✓ | ✗ | ✓ | ✓ | ✗ |

1 Can you swim, Jet? _____ Yes, I can.

2 Can you play basketball, Nick? _____

3 Can you play tennis, Kat? _____

4 Can you play hockey, Spike? _____

5 Can you skate, Nick? _____

6 Can you play football, Jet? _____

**4** Ask three children in your class.

 Can you swim?

 No, I can't.

| Name | swim | play basketball | play tennis | skate | play football | dive | ski |
|------|------|------|------|------|------|------|------|
|  |  |  |  |  |  |  |  |
|  |  |  |  |  |  |  |  |
|  |  |  |  |  |  |  |  |

## 5 Complete the sentences.

This is my family.

can't   She   run   play   can   tennis

My mum can play _____.

_____ can't swim.

My dad can _____ football.
He _____ skate.

My brother can _____ 5 km.

My sister _____ dive.

## 6 Draw and write about two people in your family.

# My star turn

My _____

_____
_____
_____
_____

My _____

**7** Read and complete the chart.

Ann, Sue and Kate are friends.

Ann can't  but she can  .

Sue can't  but she can  .

Kate can't  but she can  .

| Name | She can ... | She can't ... |
|---|---|---|
|  |  | swim |
| Ann |  |  |
|  |  |  |
|  |  |  |

**8** Answer **Yes, she can** or **No, she can't** about activity 7.

1 Can Ann swim? _____

2 Can Sue skate? _____

3 Can Kate ski? _____

**9** Listen and chant. Then listen and repeat the words.  12

Can bats in hats
Dance in the dark?
The black bat can
But the fat bat can't.

# What's in the house?

**1** Label the rooms.

| bathroom |
|---|
| kitchen |
| bedroom |
| living room |

**2** Read and draw in activity 1.

There's a little ghost in the bedroom.
There are two little ghosts in the kitchen.
There are four big ghosts in the bathroom.
There's one little ghost on the TV in the living room.

**3** Look at your drawing. Answer the questions.

Yes, there is.   No, there isn't.   Yes, there are.   No, there aren't.

1  Is there a big ghost downstairs? _____

2  Is there a little ghost upstairs? _____

3  Are there four big ghosts in the bedroom? _____

4  Are there two little ghosts in the kitchen? _____

**4** Listen and colour the bugs. 15

**5** Write the questions for activity 4.

1 Where's the _____ bug?

2 _____

3 _____

4 _____

5 _____

In the drawer.

On the TV.

Under the sofa.

Behind the plant.

In the cupboard.

**6** Write sentences about the picture in activity 4.

red   yellow   blue
black   brown   green
orange   pink

in   on
under
behind

cupboard   drawer
plant   chair
sofa   TV

The          bug is          the

1 The red bug is _____.

2 _____

3 _____

**7** | Read and circle.

This is my house / flat. There are two / three bedrooms. There's a big / little table in the dining room. In the hall / living room there's a plant. In the living room there's a sofa / chair and a TV. I like my house / flat!

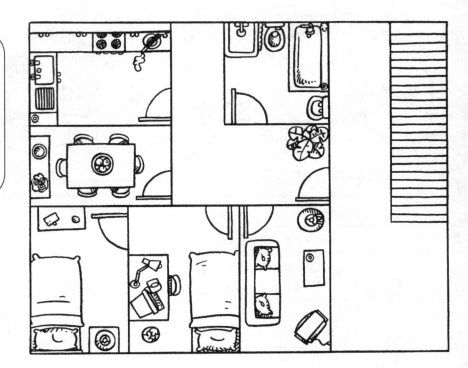

**8** | Draw and write about your flat or house.

# My star turn

★ ★ ★ ★ ★ ★ ★ ★ ★ ★ ★ ★ ★ ★ ★ ★ ★ ★ ★ ★ ★ ★ ★ ★ ★ ★ ★ ★ ★ ★

This is my _____ .

There are _____ bedrooms .

_____

There's a _____ in the _____ .

_____

_____

**9** Circle the differences in B. Then write sentences.

1 <u>In picture B, there's a pen on</u> _____.

2 _____ <u>behind the sofa.</u>

3 _____

4 _____

5 _____

**10** Listen and chant. Then listen and repeat the words. 🔊 18

There's a bug under the cupboard.
There's a bug under the clock.
There's a bug on the umbrella
And a bug under the box.

# ③ Be healthy!

**1** | Read and match.

a ☐     b ☐     c ☐

1 ( I've got a sore throat. )

2 ( I've got a headache. )

3 ( I've got a stomach ache. )

**2** | Complete the sentences.

got    headache    What's    Go    ache    I've    matter    drink

① I've _____ a stomach _____.

What's the _____?

② Please _____ this.

③ _____ the matter?

④ _____ got a _____.

_____ to bed.

**3** Read and match.

1 I've got a headache.

2 I'm tired.

3 I've got a cold.

4 I've got a stomach ache.

a Don't eat ice cream.

b Don't play loud music.

c Go to sleep.

d Don't play outside.

**4** Write instructions.

1  Go to bed.

2  _____

3  _____

4  _____

5  _____

6 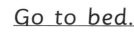 _____

**5** Complete the sentences.

| Eat | Don't | Play | lots | Ride | drink | vegetables |

Be healthy! Listen to your body!

1 Don't _____ lots of cola.

2 _____ a sport.

3 Drink _____ of water.

4 _____ lots of fruit and _____.

5 _____ eat lots of chocolate and sweets.

6 _____ a bike.

**6** Make your own poster.

## My star turn

**7** Match and write the sentences.

1 Have you …          of water.

2 I've got …          the matter?

3 Don't …          got a cold?

4 Eat lots …          eat lots of chocolate.

5 What's …          a headache.

6 Drink lots …          of fruit and vegetables.

1 <u>Have you got a cold?</u>

2 _____

3 _____

4 _____

5 _____

6 _____

**8** Listen and chant. Then listen and repeat the words. 🔊 24

Seven little spiders
All of them in bed.
Six of them are yellow.
One of them is red.

# ⏪ Review A

---

**1** Write the words.

~~swim~~   ~~cold~~   ~~drum~~   ~~bathroom~~   sofa   piano   kitchen   ski
picture   sore throat   dive   trumpet   headache   stomach ache
cupboard   run   guitar   play football   violin

| Sports | In the house | Illnesses | Musical instruments |
|---|---|---|---|
| swim | bathroom | cold | drum |
| | | | |
| | | | |
| | | | |
| | | | |

---

**2** Read, choose and match.

1. Can you skate? ☐
2. I've got a cold. ☐
3. Where's my trumpet? ☐
4. Is there a table in your kitchen? ☐

a) It's on the sofa.
b) Eat lots of fruit and vegetables.
c) Yes, I can.
d) Don't eat lots of fruit and vegetables.
e) Yes, there is.
f) No, I can't.
g) It's under the sofa.

**3** Write the sentences.

1 the | play | can | I | piano.

2 you | Can | swim?

3 got | I've | headache. | a

4 the | What's | matter?

5 three | house. | my | bedrooms | in | are | There

I | can | play | the | piano.

# Quiz time

**A** Write the words.

 1  2  3

 4  5  6

 7  8 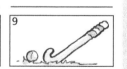 9

 10  11  12

 13  14 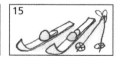 15

**B** Answer the questions.

1 Can you play the piano?

_____

2 Can you ride a bike?

_____

3 Is there a cupboard in your bedroom?

_____

4 Are there three bedrooms in your house?

_____

5 Where's the bug?

_____

High score: 15 points

High score: 10 points

Total 25

# ④ My town

**1** | Read and match.

1 café    **e**

2 clothes shop ☐

3 supermarket ☐

4 cinema ☐

5 bookshop ☐

6 sports centre ☐

**2** | Write **opposite** or **next to**.

1 The cinema is <u>opposite</u> the supermarket.

2 The café is _____ the sports centre.

3 The bookshop is _____ the clothes shop.

4 The supermarket is _____ the sports centre.

5 The clothes shop is _____ the café.

6 The sports centre is _____ the bookshop.

**3** | Write more sentences about the picture in activity 2.

1 <u>The _____</u>.

2 _____

**4** Read and complete the sentences.

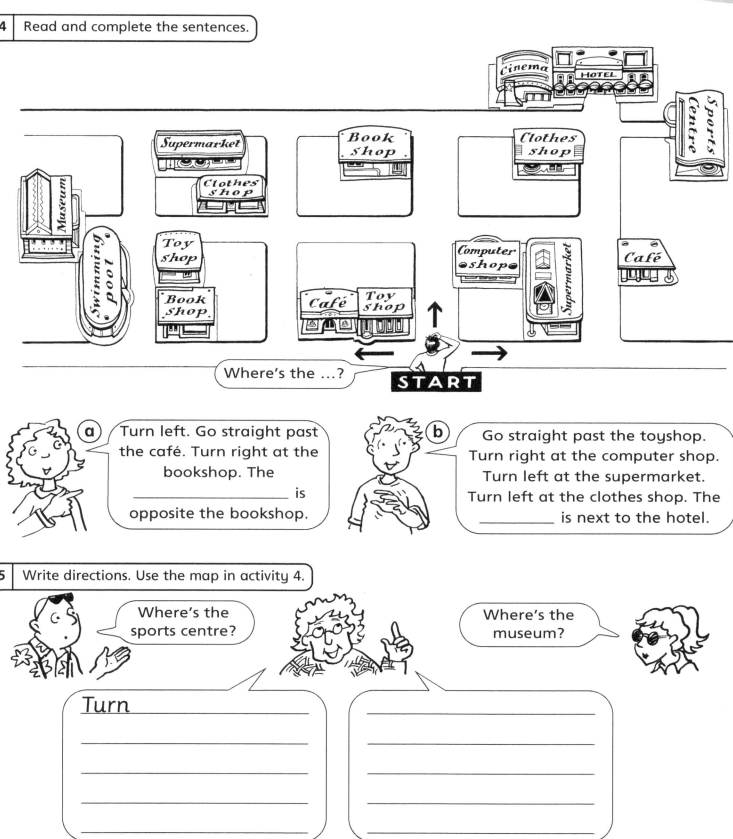

Where's the …?

**a** Turn left. Go straight past the café. Turn right at the bookshop. The _____ is opposite the bookshop.

**b** Go straight past the toyshop. Turn right at the computer shop. Turn left at the supermarket. Turn left at the clothes shop. The _____ is next to the hotel.

**5** Write directions. Use the map in activity 4.

Where's the sports centre?

Where's the museum?

Turn _____
_____
_____
_____
_____

_____
_____
_____
_____
_____

**6** Read and complete the sentences.

shops    square    river    computer    from    bookshop    opposite    little

My town

I'm _____ Bridgeton. It's a _____ town in England. There's a _____ with a statue. My school is _____ the statue.

There are good _____ in Bridgeton.

There's a great _____ shop, but there isn't a _____.

There's a _____ near the town. We can swim in it!

**7** Draw and write about your town, city or village.

# My star turn

★ ★ ★ ★ ★ ★ ★ ★ ★ ★ ★ ★ ★ ★ ★ ★ ★ ★ ★ ★ ★ ★ ★ ★ ★ ★ ★ ★ ★ ★

_____

_____

_____

_____

_____

★ ★ ★ ★ ★ ★ ★ ★ ★ ★ ★ ★ ★ ★ ★ ★ ★ ★ ★ ★ ★ ★ ★ ★ ★ ★ ★ ★ ★ ★

**8** Read and label the map.

The museum is next to the café.
The cinema is opposite the school.
The clothes shop is next to the
bookshop and the cinema.
The café is opposite the clothes shop.

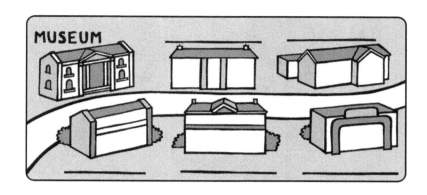

**9** Listen and chant. Then listen and repeat the words. 🔊 32

A ghost is at my window.
It's yellow, blue and brown.
There are ghosts all round my house.
There are ghosts all round the town.

# ⑤ On holiday

**1** | Read and circle **A** or **B**.

| Bug 1: | He's swimming. | A | (B) | Bug 5: | He's reading. | A | B |
| Bug 2: | She's playing football. | A | B | Bug 6: | She's writing. | A | B |
| Bug 3: | He's eating. | A | B | Bug 7: | He's dancing. | A | B |
| Bug 4: | She's diving. | A | B | Bug 8: | She's drinking. | A | B |

**2** | Answer **Yes, he/she is** or **No, he/she isn't**.

1  Is she dancing?    2  Is he drinking?    3  Is she diving?    4  Is he writing?

_____    _____    _____    _____

**3** Read and complete the sentences.

reading   I'm   doing   tennis   not   playing   you

1 What are you _____ in this picture?

I'm _____ _____ with my friend.

2 Are _____ _____ a book in this picture?

No, _____ _____.
I'm reading a comic.

**4** Draw pictures of you on holiday. Write about them.

1   2   3

1 In this picture I'm _____

2 In _____

3 _____

**5** | Write **is** or **'m** in the boxes. Then complete the sentences.

Dear Janet,

I ☐ sitting under a 🌴 _____ . Mum ☐

🏊 _____ . Sally ☐ on the beach. She ☐

playing ⚽ _____ with a friend. Dad ☐ sleeping

next to the 🏊 _____ .

I ☐ having a fantastic holiday.

Love from

Alex

**6** | You are on holiday. Write to a friend.

# My star turn

★ ★ ★ ★ ★ ★ ★ ★ ★ ★ ★ ★ ★ ★ ★ ★ ★ ★ ★ ★ ★ ★ ★ ★ ★ ★ ★ ★ ★ ★ ★ ★ ★ ★

★    <u>Dear</u> _____    ★

★ _____ ★

★ _____ ★

★ _____ ★

★ _____ ★

★ _____ ★

★ _____ ★

★ _____ ★

★ ★ ★ ★ ★ ★ ★ ★ ★ ★ ★ ★ ★ ★ ★ ★ ★ ★ ★ ★ ★ ★ ★ ★ ★ ★ ★ ★ ★ ★ ★ ★ ★ ★

**7** Read and complete the chart.

Ann, Sue and Kate are on holiday.
One girl is on the beach.
One is under a tree. One is next to the hotel.
One girl is playing tennis. One girl is reading
and one is running.
The girl next to the hotel is playing tennis.
Ann isn't reading.
Kate isn't on the beach or playing tennis.

| Name | Where is she? | What is she doing? |
|---|---|---|
| Ann | on the beach | |
| | | |
| | | reading |

**8** Listen and chant. Then listen and repeat the words.  37

Is she skipping on the beach?
Is she swimming in the sea?
No, she's reading a comic
And she's sitting next to me.

# 6 A sunny day

## 1 Read and match.

1 It's hot and sunny. `d`

2 It's raining.

3 It's cold.

4 It's windy.

5 It's snowing.

## 2 Read and match.

1 It's raining.    I've got an umbrella.

2 It's hot.    We can go to the park.

3 It's sunny.    We can play outside.

4 It's windy.    We can play with a kite.

5 It's snowing.    We've got coats.

6 It's cold.    We've got hats.

**3** Listen and draw. 🔊 41

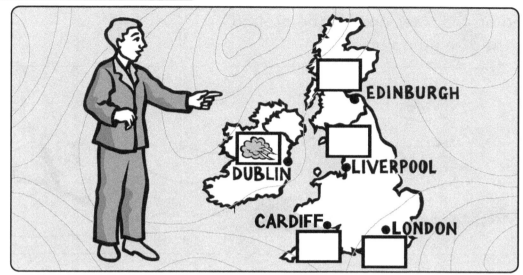

**4** Answer **Yes, it is** or **No, it isn't** about activity 3.

1  Is it windy in Dublin?  _____

2  Is it raining in Edinburgh? _____

3  Is it sunny in Cardiff?  _____

4 Is it snowing in London?  _____

5 Is it raining in Cardiff?  _____

6 Is it snowing in Edinburgh? _____

**5** Look outside the window. Complete the weather chart.

# The weather chart

1  Is it sunny now?  _____

2  Is it hot or cold today? _____

3  Is it windy today?  _____

4  Is it snowing today?  _____

5  Is it raining today?  _____

Today the weather is

_____

**6** | Make picture poems.

1   Snow is falling falling on the trees and on the ground
2   The wind is blowing the kite up up up

**7** | Make and write your own weather picture poem.

# My star turn

**8** | Complete the crossword.

ACROSS →

1  The wind is _____

3  It's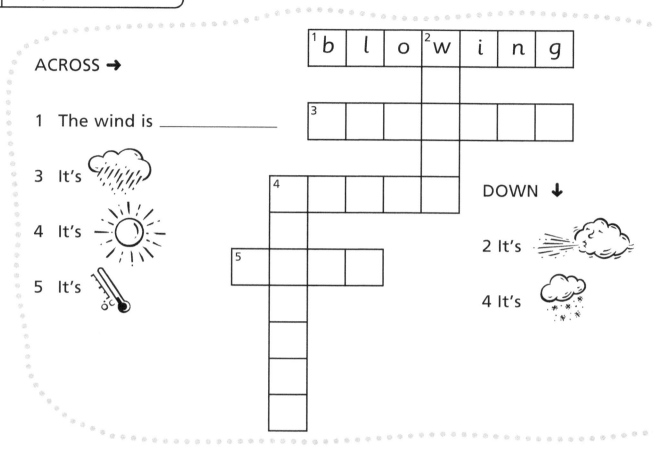

4  It's

5  It's

DOWN ↓

2 It's

4 It's

Crossword:

1 ACROSS: b l o w i n g

**9** | Listen and chant. Then listen and repeat the words. 🔊 45

It's raining in the village.
And it's very windy, too.
The weather's very bad today.
I'm very wet. Are you?

# Review B

## 1 Write the words.

café  ~~sunny~~  swimming  ~~square~~  snowing  windy
tennis  market  cold  supermarket  raining  beach
cinema  ~~hotel~~  reading

| Town | Holiday | Weather |
|------|---------|---------|
| square | hotel | sunny |
| | | |
| | | |
| | | |

## 2 Read and choose.

1. Is it raining?
2. Where's the museum?
3. Where's John?
4. What are you doing?

a) He's sitting on the beach.

b) I'm writing a letter.

c) Yes, it is.

d) It's opposite the cinema.

e) It's next to the cinema.

f) No, it isn't. It's sunny.

g) I'm reading a book.

**3** Write the sentences.

1 | right | at | Turn | bookshop. | the |

2 | you | What | doing? | are |

3 | the | past | straight | Go | café. |

4 | windy | Is | today? | it |

5 | pool. | swimming | the | She's | in |

| Turn | right | at | the | bookshop. |

# Quiz time

**A** Write the words.

 1

 2

 3

 4

 5

 6

 7

 8

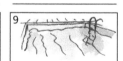 9

 10

 11

 12

 13

 14

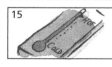 15

High score: 15 points

**B** Answer the questions.

1 What is she doing?

_____

2 What is he doing?

_____

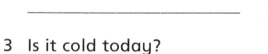

3 Is it cold today?

_____

4 Is there a market in your town?

_____

5 Is there a cinema in your town?

_____

High score: 10 points

Total $\overline{25}$

# 7 Space School

**1** Read and match.

1 It's half past twelve. **d**

2 We've got English. ☐

3 What time is it? ☐

4 We've got Maths. ☐

5 What's the matter? ☐

6 It's eleven o'clock. ☐

**2** Write the answers.    What time is it?

1

It's ten o'clock.

2

3

4

It's

5

6

7

8

9

**3** Read and match.

1 Music    d

2 Art

3 History

4 Science

5 P.E.

6 Maths

7 I.T.

a    b    c

d    e    f    g

**4** Complete your timetable. Then write sentences.

| Time | Monday | Tuesday | Wednesday | Thursday | Friday |
|---|---|---|---|---|---|
|  |  |  |  |  |  |
|  |  |  |  |  |  |
|  |  |  |  |  |  |
|  |  |  |  |  |  |

1 On Monday we've got _____ at _____ .

2 On Tuesday _____ .

3 _____

4 _____

5 _____

**5** Complete the sentences.

favourite   got   class   Maths   children   past   name   are

This is my school.

It's called Randall Primary School.

There _____ twenty-four _____ in my _____. My class

teacher's _____ is Mr Hollins. We've _____ English at half _____

nine on Monday. My _____ lessons are Art and _____.

**6** Draw and write about your school.

# My star turn

★ ★ ★ ★ ★ ★ ★ ★ ★ ★ ★ ★ ★ ★ ★ ★ ★ ★ ★ ★ ★ ★ ★ ★ ★ ★ ★ ★ ★

This is _____

There are _____ in my class.

My class teacher's _____.

We've got English _____.

My favourite lessons _____

_____.

My class

★ ★ ★ ★ ★ ★ ★ ★ ★ ★ ★ ★ ★ ★ ★ ★ ★ ★ ★ ★ ★ ★ ★ ★ ★ ★ ★ ★ ★

**7** | Read and write the names.

**Peter**

| DAY | LESSON | | |
|-----|--------|--|--|
| Monday | | Hello | 8×4: |
| Tuesday | | ♪ | |
| Wednesday | 8×4: | | Hello |
| Thursday | | 1066 | ♪ |
| Friday | | Hello | |

**Jen**

| DAY | LESSON | | |
|-----|--------|--|--|
| Monday | Hello | 1066 | |
| Tuesday | | 8×4: | ♪ |
| Wednesday | | ♪ | 1066 |
| Thursday | Hello | 8×4: | |
| Friday | | | Hello |

**Liz**

| DAY | LESSON | | |
|-----|--------|--|--|
| Monday | | 8×4: | Hello |
| Tuesday | 8×4: | | 1066 |
| Wednesday | Hello | 8×4: | |
| Thursday | ♪ | Hello | 8×4: |
| Friday | 1066 | | |

**1**
On Friday we've got Art.
On Wednesday we've got Maths.
On Monday we've got English.
On Tuesday we've got History.

Name: _____

**2**
On Wednesday we've got Science.
On Thursday we've got P.E.
On Tuesday we've got Music.
On Friday we've got Swimming.

Name: _____

**8** | Listen and chant. Then listen and repeat the words.  52

Good morning. Where's your ruler?
Good morning. Where's your book?
Good morning. Now it's time for school.
Please sit up and look!

# 8 What's on TV?

**1** | Read, match and write.

~~action films~~  comedies   music programmes   animal programmes   quizzes
sports programmes   cartoons   science fiction films

a    b   c   d

action films _____   _____   _____

e    f    g 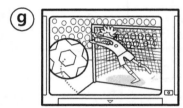   h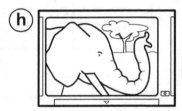

_____   _____   _____   _____

**2** | Write six sentences.

1  I like _____ .   4  I _____ quizzes. _____

2  I don't like _____ .   5  _____

3  I _____ comedies. _____   6  _____

**3** | Write five favourite TV programmes. Ask two friends.

| TV programmes | Friend 1: _____ | Friend 2: _____ |
|---|---|---|
|  |  |  |
|  |  |  |
|  |  |  |
|  |  |  |
|  |  |  |

Do you like quizzes?

Yes, I do. They're great!

No, I don't. They're boring.

**4** Listen and play. 🔊 56

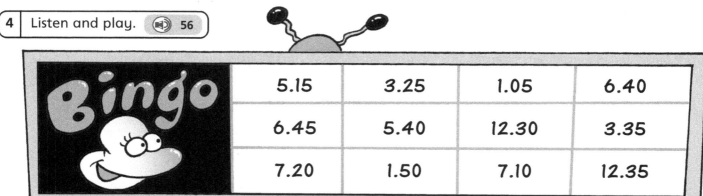

| 5.15 | 3.25 | 1.05 | 6.40 |
| 6.45 | 5.40 | 12.30 | 3.35 |
| 7.20 | 1.50 | 7.10 | 12.35 |

**5** Listen and match. 🔊 57

1 ☐

2 ☐

3 ☐

4 ☐

ⓐ The Top Ten

ⓑ Winter sports

ⓒ The Animal Hour

ⓓ Oh no, Frank!

**6** Listen and complete the sentences. 🔊 58

1 ( Ice hockey is on Channel _____ at _____. )

2 ( 'Oh no, Frank!' is on Channel _____ at _____. )

3 ( 'Animal Hour' is on Channel _____ at _____. )

4 ( 'The Top Ten' is on Channel _____ at _____. )

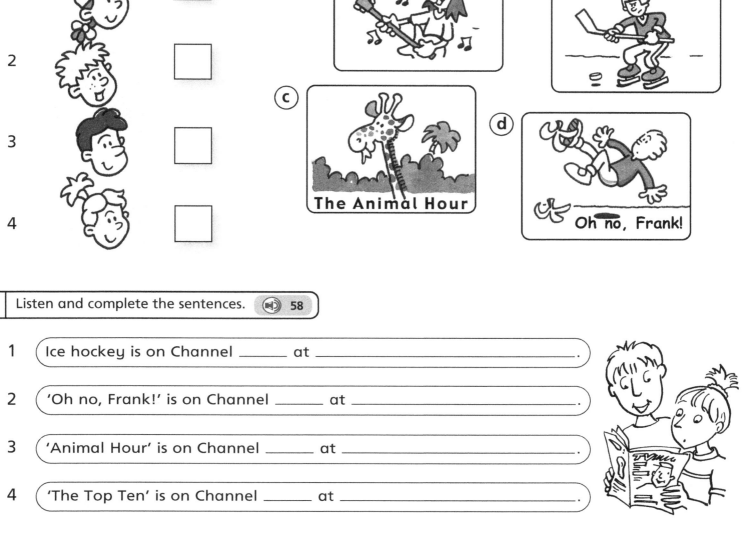

---

**7** | Match the questions and answers.

1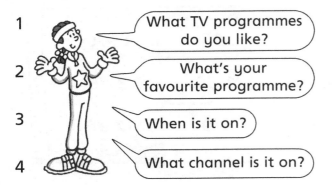
What TV programmes do you like?

2
What's your favourite programme?

3
When is it on?

4
What channel is it on?

☐ **a** It's on Channel 1.

☐ **b** I like comedies.

☐ **c** It's on Monday at 7.40.

☐ **d** My favourite programme is 'L and H'.

---

**8** | Circle the correct word.

My favourite TV programme is 'Twenty Questions'. It's a quiz / comedy. It's on Tuesday / Thursday at half past six / eight. It's on Channel 1 / 4.

Twenty Questions

CHANNEL 1

TUESDAY
25
JULY

---

**9** | Write about your favourite TV programme.

# My star turn

My favourite TV programme is _____.

_____

It's a _____

_____

_____

**10** Read and answer.

1 What time is the quiz on?

<u>It's on at</u> _____ .

5 What channel is the science fiction film on?

_____

2 What channel is the comedy on?

_____

6 What time is it on?

_____

3 What time is the pop music programme on?

_____

4 What channel is it on?

_____

| Channel 1 | Channel 2 |
|---|---|
| **6.05** The Top Ten | **6.10** Amazing Animals |
| **6.45** Film: | **6.55** Cartoons |
| Space School | **7.10** The Comedy Hour |
| **9.15** News | **8.10** Film: |
| **9.30** Football | My Favourite Dog |
| | **9.40** Ten Questions |
| | Britain's favourite quiz. |

**11** Listen and chant. Then listen and repeat the words.  62

On Thursday at four thirty,
There's a programme on TV.
It's a great cartoon with a purple bird
In a pink and purple tree!

# (9) My free time

**1** Complete the answers.

What do you do in your free time?

| play | read | watch | ride | play |

1 ( I _____ a book. )

2 ( I _____ tennis. )

3 ( I _____ my bike. )

4 ( I _____ TV. )

5 ( I _____ football. )

**2** Look and write the days.

| Monday | Tuesday | Wednesday | Thursday | Friday | Saturday | Sunday |
|--------|---------|-----------|----------|--------|----------|--------|
|        |         |           |          |        |          |        |

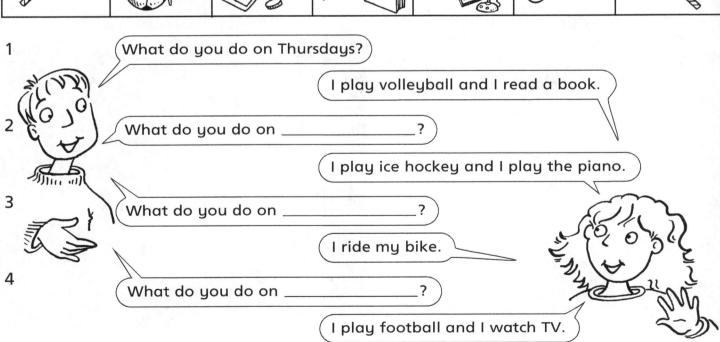

1 ( What do you do on Thursdays? )

( I play volleyball and I read a book. )

2 ( What do you do on _____? )

( I play ice hockey and I play the piano. )

3 ( What do you do on _____? )

( I ride my bike. )

4 ( What do you do on _____? )

( I play football and I watch TV. )

**3** Write the letters and words in the boxes.

|  | I go ... |  | I play ... |
|---|---|---|---|
| h | running | a | football |
|  |  |  |  |
|  |  |  |  |
|  |  |  |  |

**4** Look at the room. Answer **Yes, I do** or **No, I don't**.

1  Do you play table tennis in your free time? — Yes, I do.

2 Do you go fishing?

_____

3 Do you listen to music?

_____

4 Do you play basketball?

_____

5 Do you read comics?

_____

6 Do you play computer games?

_____

**5** | Read and circle the correct words.

Hello. I'm **your** /**my** new penfriend. My name is James. I'm **at/from** Chester in England. I've **got/have** lots of hobbies. I **play/go** swimming on Mondays and I **go/play** basketball **on/in** Fridays. I **read/ride** my bike after school. On Sundays I **play/do** the guitar. What do you **be/do** in your free time?

Best wishes,
James

**6** | Write a letter to a penfriend.

# My star turn

★ ★ ★ ★ ★ ★ ★ ★ ★ ★ ★ ★ ★ ★ ★ ★ ★ ★ ★ ★ ★ ★ ★ ★ ★ ★ ★ ★

Hello. My name is _____.

I'm from _____.

I _____

_____

Best wishes, _____

_____

★ ★ ★ ★ ★ ★ ★ ★ ★ ★ ★ ★ ★ ★ ★ ★ ★ ★ ★ ★ ★ ★ ★ ★ ★ ★ ★ ★

**7** Read and match.

1 ☐

> On Saturdays I read a book and I go fishing. On Sundays I play the drums.

2 ☐

> I listen to music after school. On Fridays I go swimming and I play the violin.

(a) (b) (c) (d) (e) (f)

**8** Listen and chant. Then listen and repeat the words. 🔊 67

On Saturday morning, I run and run.
I go to the park and I have fun.
On Sunday morning, I don't run.
I read a comic and I play the drums.

# Review C

## 1 Write the words.

go shopping    English    comedies    ~~Maths~~    music programmes    films
History    ~~quizzes~~    ~~go fishing~~    Art    cartoons    play table tennis    P.E.
play computer games    watch TV    Music channel    read a book

| School | TV | Hobbies |
|---|---|---|
| Maths | quizzes | go fishing |
|  |  |  |
|  |  |  |
|  |  |  |
|  |  |  |
|  |  |  |

## 2 Read and choose.

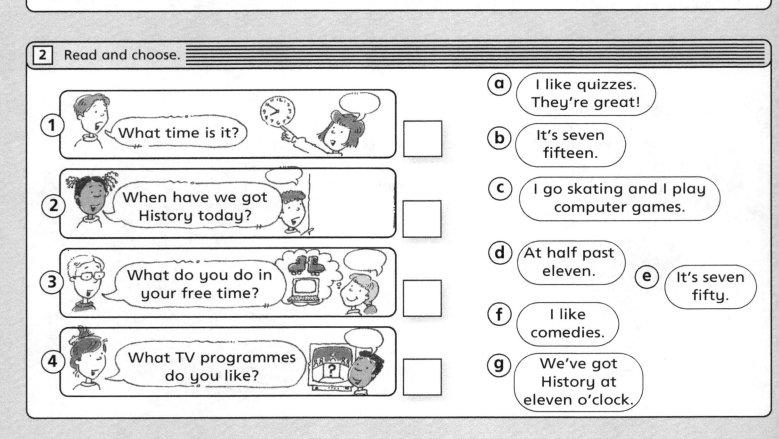

1. What time is it? ☐

2. When have we got History today? ☐

3. What do you do in your free time? ☐

4. What TV programmes do you like? ☐

(a) I like quizzes. They're great!

(b) It's seven fifteen.

(c) I go skating and I play computer games.

(d) At half past eleven.

(e) It's seven fifty.

(f) I like comedies.

(g) We've got History at eleven o'clock.

**3** Write the sentences.

1 | it? | is | time | What |

2 | past | half | It's | twelve. |

3 | programmes? | like | you | music | Do |

4 | got | When | we | have | Art? |

5 | shopping? | you | go | Do |

| What | time | is | it? |

# Quiz time

**A** Write the words.

 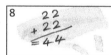 

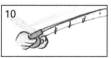  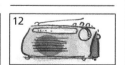

**B** Answer the questions.

1 Have you got Art today?

_____

2 What is your favourite lesson?

_____

3 What TV programmes do you like?

_____

4 What do you do on Saturdays?

_____

5 Do you go shopping in your free time?

_____

High score: 15 points

High score: 10 points

Total $\overline{25}$

# 10 Amazing animals

**1** Complete the sentences.

| lion | gorilla | frog | penguin | whale | crocodile |

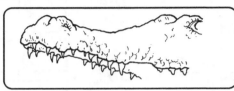

1 This is a _____ .  2 This is a _____ .  3 This is a _____ .

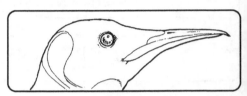

4 This is a _____ .  5 This is a _____ .  6 This is a _____ .

**2** Match and write sentences.

1 A penguin eats ...          fish and meat.

2 A gorilla eats ...          fish.

3 A frog eats ...             leaves.

4 A lion eats ...             insects.

5 A crocodile eats ...        meat.

1  <u>A penguin eats fish.</u> _____

2  _____

3  _____

4  _____

5  _____

**3** Read and write the names.

snowy owl   penguin   crocodile   lion   polar bear   fruit bat   hippo   elephant

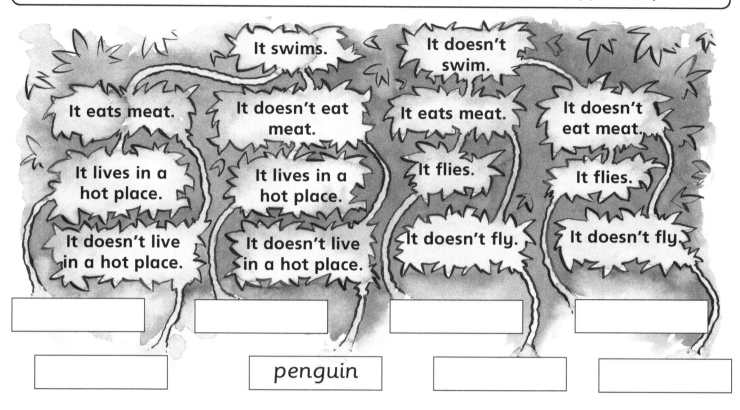

It swims.

It doesn't swim.

It eats meat.

It doesn't eat meat.

It eats meat.

It doesn't eat meat.

It lives in a hot place.

It lives in a hot place.

It flies.

It flies.

It doesn't live in a hot place.

It doesn't live in a hot place.

It doesn't fly.

It doesn't fly.

penguin

**4** Answer **Yes, it does** or **No, it doesn't**.

1 Does it swim?
Yes, it does.

2 Does it swim?
_____

3 Does it live in a hot place?
_____

4 Does it fly?
_____

5 Does it live in a hot place?
_____

6 Does it eat fish and meat?
_____

7 Does it fly?
_____

8 Does it eat meat?
_____

**5** Match the questions and answers.

1 Where does the hippo live? ☐     a No, it doesn't.

2 Does it live in a hot place? ☐     b Yes, it does.

3 Does it eat meat? ☐     c It lives in rivers.

4 What does it eat? ☐     d It eats plants.

**6** Read and circle.

My favourite animal is the hippo. It lives in rivers / the sea. It's big / small and grey. It lives / doesn't live in a hot place. It eats meat / plants.

**7** Draw and write about your favourite animal.

# My star turn

My _____

_____

_____

_____

_____

**8** Look and write.

A giraffe doesn't swim!

1

A giraffe
doesn't swim.

4

2

5

3

6

**9** Listen and chant. Then listen and repeat the words.  75

Where? Where is the polar bear?
I can't see it here.
I can't see it there.
It's really, really big
And it's got white hair.
Look! Here it is.
It's sitting in my chair.

I think Unit 10 was ★ OK ★★ Good ★★★ Great

**1** | Read and circle.

The first horse is/was alive 50,000,000 years ago. It was/had very small. It was/has 50 centimetres tall. It has/had four toes on its front feet. It had/was three toes on its back feet. Today the horse is/was very different.

**2** | Complete the sentences with **was** or **had**.

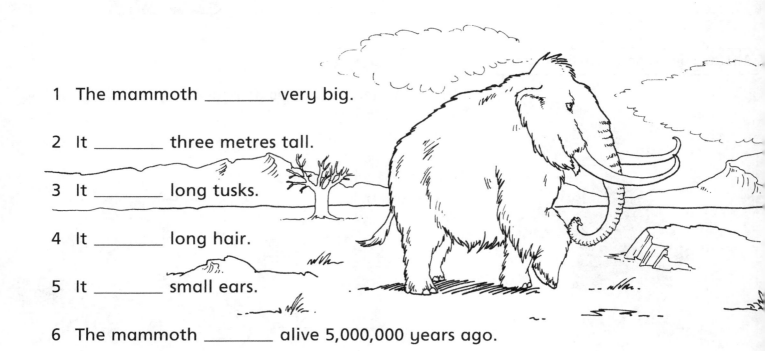

1  The mammoth _____ very big.

2  It _____ three metres tall.

3  It _____ long tusks.

4  It _____ long hair.

5  It _____ small ears.

6  The mammoth _____ alive 5,000,000 years ago.

**3** Complete the sentences. Then match them with the picture.

| sharp | short | big | short | ~~sharp~~ | long | strong |

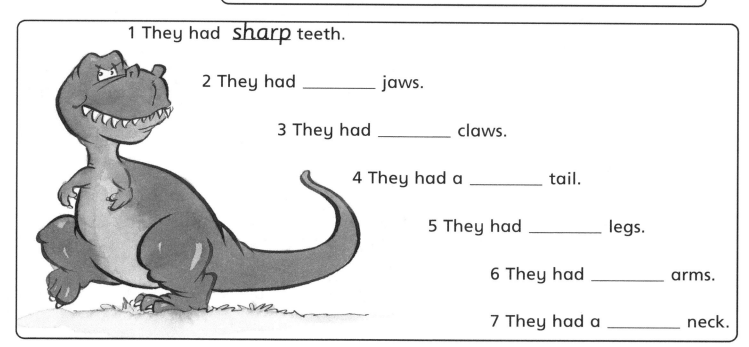

1 They had **sharp** teeth.

2 They had _____ jaws.

3 They had _____ claws.

4 They had a _____ tail.

5 They had _____ legs.

6 They had _____ arms.

7 They had a _____ neck.

**4** Write about pictures A and B.

(A)

(B)

1 <u>Dinosaur A had four legs.</u>    1 _____

2 <u>It had</u> _____.    2 _____

3 <u>It was</u> _____.    3 _____

**5** Read and write the sentences.

(1) Campsognathus

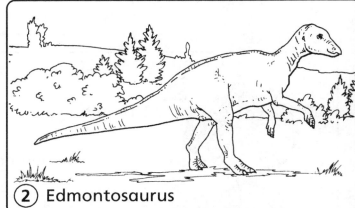

(2) Edmontosaurus

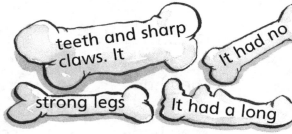

teeth and sharp claws. It

It had no

tail. It had sharp

was a meat eater.

strong legs

It had a long

teeth. It was a plant

eater. It had two

and two arms.

1 _____

2 _____

**6** Draw your own dinosaur and write about it.

# My star turn

Dinosaur: _____

This dinosaur _____

_____

_____

**7** | Match and write.

1 The mammoth's tusks .. | C |          a had sharp teeth and claws.

2 The first horse … | |                    b are big.

3 The T. Rex … | |                         c were very long.

4 The pteranadon … | |                    d had no teeth.

5 Now an elephant … | |                   e is three metres tall.

6 An elephant's ears … | |                f was small.

1 _____    4 _____

2 _____    5 _____

3 _____    6 _____

**8** | Listen and chant. Then listen and repeat the words. 🔊 82

Three big mammoths
With long tusks, too.
One mammoth was thirsty.
Then there were two.

Two big mammoths
Having lots of fun.
One mammoth was hungry.
Then there was one!

I think Unit 11 was ★ OK ★★ Good ★★★ Great

**1** | Read, match and write.

a Is stone soup good? ☐

b Please give us some food. ☐

c Are you making a fire? ☐

d Here are some potatoes for the soup. ☐

e What are you doing? ☐

f Yes, it is. ☐

g Yes, I am. ☐

**6** What are you making?

**7**

h Look. He's going to the shop.

i Let's eat the soup!

**8**

**9**

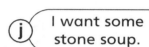j I want some stone soup.

k It's stone soup with potatoes.

l I like stone soup!

**10** I'm sorry. There's no soup now.

**11**

m Here's a stone. Now you can make stone soup!

**2** | Complete the crossword.

# Mammoth crossword

**Across**

4

7 You go _____ in a swimming pool.

9  It flies and it eats meat.

10 This animal is big and it lives in the sea.

11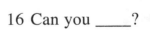

15 You watch films here.

16 Can you _____?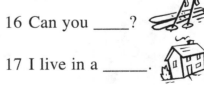

17 I live in a _____.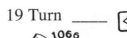

18 Go to _____.

19 Turn _____

21

22 _____ lots of vegetables.

23 My favourite programme is on _____ 2.

24

26 10

27 I don't live in a city or a town. I live in a small _____

28 Apples and bananas are _____

**Down**

1

2

3 I'm scared of dinosaurs. They're _____!

4 It's _____.

5 Can you _____ a bike?

6 There's a cooker in my _____ .

7 I'm ill. I've got a _____ .

8 Lions eat _____ .

12  ..

13

14

16

20 On Sundays I go _____ in the woods.

25

---

**3** | Listen and chant. 🔊 87

One, two, three, four.
Now I'm running to the door.
Five, six, seven, eight.
Summer time is really great!

Nine, ten.
Goodbye, my friend!
It's time to go.
This is the end!

---

I think Unit 12 was ★ OK ★★ Good ★★★ Great

# Quiz time

## A Write the words.

1  _____

2  _____

3  _____

4  _____

5  go _____

6  _____

7  _____

8 _____

9 _____

10 _____

11 _____

12  _____

13 _____

14 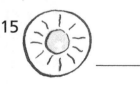 _____

15 _____

## B Answer about you.

1 Can you play a musical instrument?

_____

2 How many bedrooms are there in your house/flat?

_____

3 Can you dive?

_____

4 Is there a museum in your town?

_____

5 How many children are there in your class?

_____

6 Do you like sports programmes on TV?

_____

7 What's your favourite animal?

_____

8 Does your favourite animal live in a hot place?

_____

9 What do you do after school?

_____

10 What do you do on Saturdays?

_____

High score: 15 points

High score: 10 points

Total 25

# Certificate

This is to certify that

_____

has completed Level 2 of Chit Chat.

Signed _____ (teacher)

## Congratulations!

## You're a Superstar!

# Picture dictionary

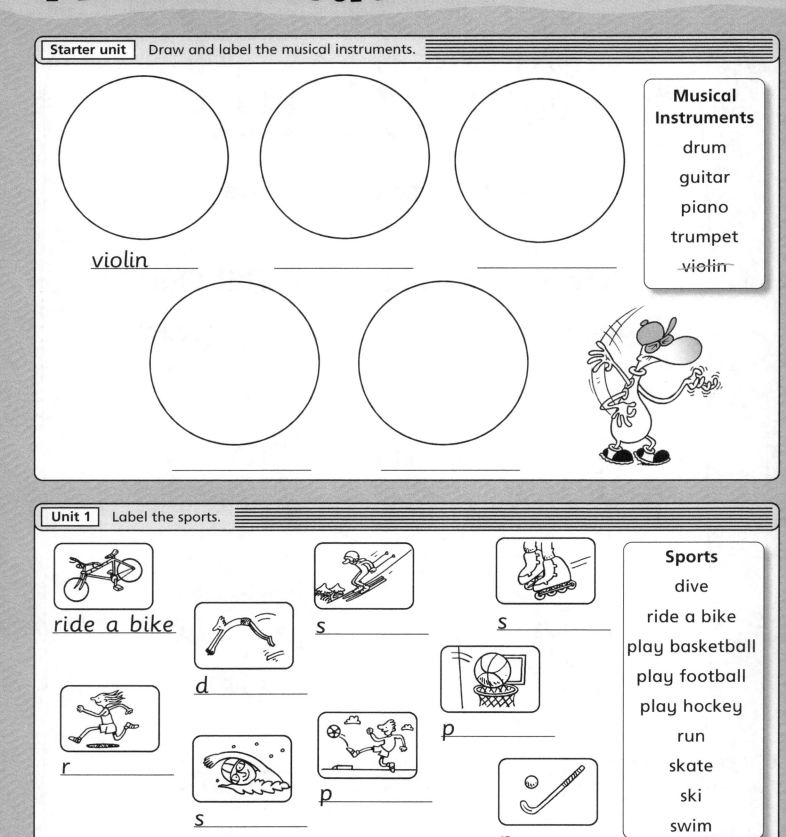

**Starter unit**  Draw and label the musical instruments.

violin _____  _____  _____

_____  _____

**Musical Instruments**
drum
guitar
piano
trumpet
~~violin~~

**Unit 1**  Label the sports.

ride a bike

d _____

s _____

s _____

p _____

r _____

s _____

p _____

p _____

**Sports**
dive
ride a bike
play basketball
play football
play hockey
run
skate
ski
swim

**Rooms**

bathroom
bedroom
dining room
hall
kitchen
living room

**Furniture**

bath
bed
chair
cooker
cupboard
drawer
picture
plant
sofa
table

**Unit 3**   Label the illnesses.

**Illnesses**

a cold
a headache
a sore throat
a stomach ache

## Unit 4 | Label the places and shops.

### Places and shops

bookshop  café  castle  ~~church~~  cinema  clothes shop  hotel  museum  park
sports centre  square  statue  supermarket  ~~swimming pool~~  ~~toy shop~~

toy shop

church

swimming pool

## Unit 5 | Label and draw the activities.

      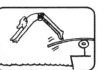

_____  _____  _____  _____

_____  _____  _____  _____

_____  _____  _____  _____

### Activities

| | |
|---|---|
| dancing | running |
| diving | sitting |
| drinking | skipping |
| eating | sleeping |
| jumping | swimming |
| reading | writing |

**Cities**

Cardiff

Dublin

Edinburgh

Liverpool

London

Oxford

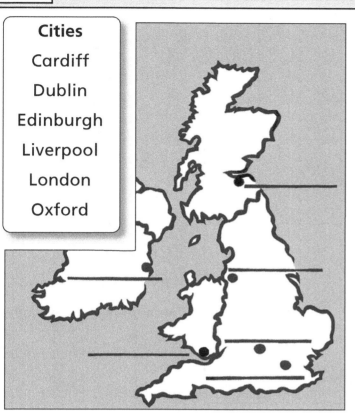

**Weather**

It's cold

It's hot

It's raining

It's snowing

It's sunny

It's windy

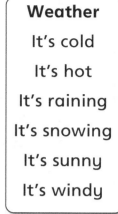

Unit 7 | Complete the timetable. Write the lessons.

| Monday | Tuesday | Wednesday | Thursday | Friday | Lessons |
|--------|---------|-----------|----------|--------|---------|
| | | | | | Art |
| | | | | | ~~Break~~ |
| Break | | | | | English |
| | | | | | History |
| | | | | | I.T. |
| Lunch | | | | | ~~Lunch~~ |
| | | | | | Maths |
| | | | | | Music |
| | | | | | P.E. |
| | | | | | Science |

65

## TV Guide

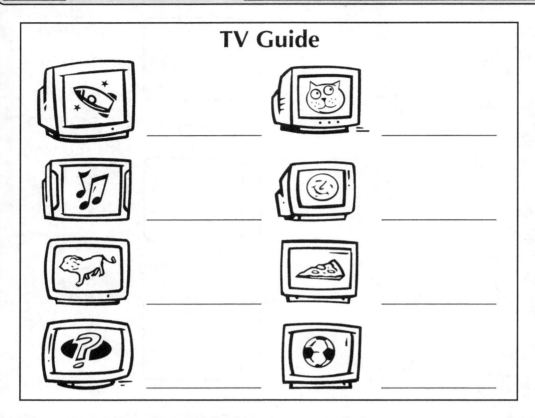

**TV programmes**

animal programmes

cartoons

comedies

food programmes

music programmes

quizzes

science fiction films

sports programmes

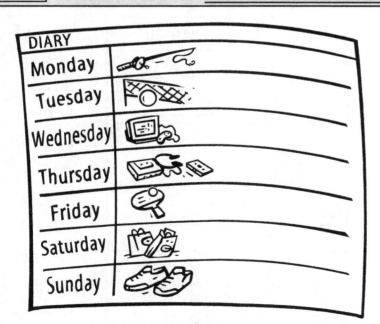

**Hobbies**

go fishing          play computer

go running             games

go shopping        play table tennis

go skating          play volleyball

go swimming       read a book

listen to music

| Unit 10 | Choose and write. |
| --- | --- |

| Animal | Food | Hot place |
| --- | --- | --- |
| *giraffe* | *leaves* | ✓ |
| | | ☐ |
| | | ☐ |
| | | ☐ |
| | | ☐ |
| | | ☐ |
| | | ☐ |
| | | ☐ |
| | | ☐ |
| | | ☐ |
| | | ☐ |
| | | ☐ |

**Animals**

crocodile
elephant
frog
fruit bat
~~giraffe~~
gorilla
hippo
lion
penguin
polar bear
snowy owl
whale

**Food**

fish
fruit
insects
~~leaves~~
meat
meat and fish
plants

| Unit 11 | Label the dinosaurs. |
| --- | --- |

a long tail

**Parts of body**

a long neck
~~a long tail~~
a small head
big jaws
sharp claws
sharp teeth
short arms
strong legs

name | favourite | colour | Red | pizza | violin | Yes | No | tennis

ghost | two | kitchen | cupboard | green | bug | bedroom | upstairs

downstairs | bed | sport | cinema | café | Mum | tennis | cold | windy

snowing | sunny | wind | blowing | raining | nine | o'clock | half | past

eleven | Monday | Art | class | pet | great | scary | boring | twenty-five

channel | time | book | volleyball | fishing | free | Saturday | shopping

plants | meat | fish | fly | whale | giraffe | small | long | hair

meat eater | tail | programme | 's | 's | 's | s | s | . | ? | ?

Play does

Please Go Are Is Can Where Who What

Do Don't

My They we've We've can't can play

next to left right Turn isn't is the The On

doesn't from outside behind to on in past straight

it swim you I this your she he She He opposite

were was eat read drink got do are is there

, , 's 's ing ing 're 'm ? like no at had

# OXFORD
UNIVERSITY PRESS

Great Clarendon Street, Oxford OX2 6DP

Oxford University Press is a department of the University of Oxford.
It furthers the University's objective of excellence in research, scholarship,
and education by publishing worldwide in

Oxford  New York

Auckland  Cape Town  Dar es Salaam  Hong Kong  Karachi
Kuala Lumpur  Madrid  Melbourne  Mexico City  Nairobi
New Delhi  Shanghai  Taipei  Toronto

With offices in

Argentina  Austria  Brazil  Chile  Czech Republic  France  Greece
Guatemala  Hungary  Italy  Japan  Poland  Portugal  Singapore
South Korea  Switzerland  Thailand  Turkey  Ukraine  Vietnam

OXFORD and OXFORD ENGLISH are registered trade marks of
Oxford University Press in the UK and in certain other countries

ISBN: 978 0 19 437836 9

Printed in Great Britain by Ashford Colour Press Ltd.

This book is printed on paper from certified and well-managed sources.

ACKNOWLEDGEMENTS

*Illustrations*

Adrian Barclay pp. 9, 15, 17, 18, 26, 28, 31, 32, 34, 35, 37, 46, 58, 59, 63, 65, 66
Kathy Baxendale pp. 40, 44, 50, 51
Gary Boller pp. 4, 5, 6, 11, 13, 19, 24, 31, 33, 39, 47, 62, 63, 65
Andy Cooke pp. 2, 3, 7, 25, 39, 40, 50
Strawberrie Donnelly p. 30
Jackie East pp. 6, 7, 9, 11, 21, 28, 39, 42, 43
Neil Gower pp. 21, 22
Teri Gower pp. 13, 18, 27, 32, 36, 45, 46
Karen Hiscock pp. 48, 52, 54
Martin Impey pp. 5, 9, 10, 14, 17, 19, 23, 27, 31, 33, 37, 41, 45, 47, 49, 54 59,
51, 53, 54, 55, 58, 60, 67
Andy Peters pp. 8, 12, 12, 24, 42, 43, 62, 63, 64
Mark Ruffle pp. 16, 38, 48
Jane Smith pp. 20, 23, 29, 64, 65
Tom Sperling pp. 56, 57

*Cover illustration*: Gary Boller and Andy Cooke

The publishers would like to thank all the teachers who have commented on
the course at various stages of its development. In particular, Coralyn
Bradshaw, Leonor Corradi, Joan Hood, Dana Hurtová, Catia Longo, Alicia
López Martin, Debi Moss, Sabina Pazderová, Silvia Ronchetti, and the
teachers and supervisors of the state schools in Ciudad Autónoma de Buenos
Aires. We would also like to thank all the teachers who have given us
valuable feedback on **Chatterbox** over the years

The publishers advise that work involving cutting and sticking should be
carried out under the supervision of an adult